Baking With Quinoa

Healthier Bread, Muffin, Cookie and Cake Recipes

Sarah Clarence

ISBN-13: 978-1478206644
ISBN-10: 1478206640

First Printing, 2012

Printed in the United States of America

Disclaimer/Legal Notice
The information presented represents the view of the author as of the day of publication. Due to the rate at which conditions change, the author reserves the right to alter and update her opinions based on new conditions.

This book is for informational and entertainment purposes only. While every attempt was made to accurately state the information provided here, neither the author nor her affiliates or publisher assume any responsibility for errors, inaccuracies or omissions. Please consult your doctor before starting any new diet or exercise program. Any slights to people or organizations are unintentional.

Baking With Quinoa

Healthier Bread, Muffin, Cookie and Cake Recipes

Other Books By Sarah Clarence

Amazon Best Sellers:
Quinoa Recipes For Weight Loss

Quinoa Salad and Side Dishes

Table of Contents

Introduction

Thank you for picking up a copy of *Baking With Quinoa: Healthier Bread, Muffin, Cookie and Cake Recipes*. This book came about because of the overwhelming response that I received after publishing my first book, *Quinoa Recipes For Weight Loss.*

Many of my readers wrote to me to tell me how much they enjoyed that book and the recipes in them. Many people had never heard of quinoa before and I was delighted to hear so many people say that they felt so much better, so much more energetic after incorporating quinoa into their diet. And many people asked me if I had any more recipes for some of their favorite foods: breads, muffins, cookies and cakes.

So, I created this book of some of my family's favorites. There are so many things I love about quinoa, but one of the things I like best is that it is so easy to use in many of my favorite recipes. As you become more comfortable with quinoa, I urge you to experiment and see which recipes of yours you can make healthier and more nutrient-rich, by adding quinoa.

Let's get started!

Using Quinoa to Make Healthier Baked Goods

Quinoa, pronounced keen-wah, is quickly becoming popular worldwide. Quinoa is often considered a grain and is used in many recipes in the same way as grains, but it is actually a seed. It contains many nutrients and can be used to make favorite dishes healthier than ever.

Quinoa is an extremely versatile food. It can be used in vegetable dishes, in place of rice, in breakfast cereals or main dishes. Many people, however, don't think about using quinoa for baking.

Using quinoa while baking will add additional nutrition to your baked goods, making them healthier than using all-purpose or wheat flour alone. Quinoa is a complete protein, containing all nine essential amino acids. One cup of quinoa contains about 200 calories, 40 grams of carbohydrates, 8 grams of protein, 3.5 grams of fat, and 5 grams of fiber. Quinoa is also a good source of protein.

Quinoa also contains phosphorus, manganese, magnesium, and lysine, which is essential for tissue growth and repair. It is a good source of magnesium, which is a mineral that helps to relax blood vessels, which can help reduce the frequency and severity of migraines.

Using quinoa in your baked goods will not only add a new texture and taste to your favorite desserts, but it will make them healthier as well, by adding a ton of nutrients.

Types of Quinoa

There are three main types of quinoa that are sold commercially. Gold quinoa is the most common type of quinoa sold. It is this quinoa that I use most often when baking. It is fluffier and lighter than the other types of quinoa and mixes well into recipes.

Red quinoa is higher in protein, calories and fiber than gold. However, it has a more bitter taste than gold and so is better used in salads and vegetable dishes than in baking. Black quinoa is the most difficult type of quinoa to find. It adds sweetness and crunch to recipes and I prefer to add this type of quinoa to cereal dishes.

In this recipe book, I use gold quinoa throughout.

How to Use Quinoa For Baking

It is a good idea to rinse quinoa seeds with water prior to baking. This is because the quinoa seeds have a natural coating that has a bitter taste. Commercial processes remove much of this residue, but it is still a good idea to rinse the seeds in cold water, until the water runs clear, to make sure the process is complete.

After rinsing the seeds, bring a pot of one part quinoa and two parts water to a boil. Then cover the pot and simmer for fifteen minutes. When you see the sprouts popping out, you'll know the quinoa is just about ready. At this point, stir the quinoa so all the water gets absorbed.

In all of the recipes in this book that call for quinoa, I use uncooked quinoa and give the directions for cooking the quinoa. You may come across other recipes that call for cooked quinoa. It is important to know that quinoa, like rice, cooks up to a greater volume. One-fourth cup of quinoa cooks up to 1 cup of cooked quinoa. So, if you find a recipe that calls for 2 cups cooked quinoa, you will cook 1/2 cup of uncooked quinoa to yield the two cups of cooked quinoa.

Substituting Wheat Flour in Baking

If you want the nutritional value of quinoa or need dishes that are gluten-free, you can, to a degree substitute all-purpose flour for quinoa flour. Quinoa flour has a different consistency than all-purpose flour and is not a 'rising' flour that many baked-goods need, so what I like to do is to substitute only a portion of the flour requirement with quinoa, to ensure that the finished product retains the desired structure. In most of the recipes in this book, I combine quinoa flour with wheat flour or use quinoa and wheat flour. In this way, my baked goods have both the nutritional value and a good consistency.

If you need gluten-free recipes you can substitute wheat flour with a gluten-free flour mix. A good one on the market is King Arthur Gluten Free Multi-Purpose Flour. If you prefer to make a gluten-free flour mix yourself you can do so by mixing 1 cup rice flour, 1/2 cup potato starch and 1/4 tapioca flour.

Preparing Store Bought Quinoa Flour

Many people use store-bought quinoa flour as is, but I have found that when I do that my baked goods have a grassy taste. Not that I have ever eaten grass...but you get the idea. To offset this I bake quinoa flour prior to use. I believe this extra step is well worth it. If you don't, it can help to mix quinoa flour with another flour such as all-purpose or wheat flour. This will minimize the grassy taste.

To bake quinoa flour, follow the following steps:

> Preheat oven to 215 (F.)
>
> Gently pour the bag of quinoa flour onto a cookie sheet (or several), lined with parchment paper. It is important to make sure the layer of flour is no deeper than 1/4" so you may need to use several cookie sheets.
>
> Place the cookie sheets in the preheated oven for two hours. Remove the cookie sheets from oven and allow to cool. Place the flour in airtight container.
>
> You can store the containers in the freezer for several months if you are not planning to use flour soon. Flour that you plan to use more quickly can be placed in an airtight container the refrigerator. Due to the high fat content in quinoa, it can turn rancid quickly.

Some store bought quinoa flour states that it is pre-toasted. I have found that even this needs to be toasted again if not mixed with other flour such as all-purpose or rice flour, but you may feel differently. Give it a try!

Making Your Own Quinoa Flour

Quinoa can be ground into flour. Using quinoa flour will give the baked goods a unique flavor and texture.

One cup of quinoa grains will yield about 3/4 cup of quinoa flour. It is important to not make too much quinoa flour ahead of time because it will become rancid quickly. You can freeze quinoa flour in an airtight container to extend its shelf life, or refrigerate quinoa in an airtight container if you plan on using it more quickly.

> Rinse the quinoa seeds thoroughly. Rinse it several times until the rinse water no longer has a soapy residue. Although most commercial quinoa grains are pre-washed, it is a good idea to rinse them again.
>
> In a non-stick pan, on low heat, sauté the quinoa seeds until they turn golden. They will also begin to pop.
>
> Remove the toasted quinoa seeds from the pan, and set aside to cool.
>
> Once the quinoa seeds have cooled, put them in a blender. Blend the quinoa seeds until it has reached the consistency of cornmeal (it is easier to use at this consistency than if you continue to blend it to the point where it is like traditional flour).

I have found that when I make quinoa flour is this way, it does not have the grassy taste that commercial quinoa flour has. However, if you feel differently, you can always toast the flour as described in the section **Preparing Store Bought Quinoa Flour**.

Store the flour by putting it in an airtight container and keep in a refrigerator until you are ready to use it. Due to the high fat content of quinoa, the flour does not keep long.

Storing Quinoa

It is important to store quinoa correctly, as quinoa does not keep long. By keeping it in an airtight plastic or glass container it will keep the grain from absorbing moisture and odors. By storing it in the refrigerator or freezer, it will stay fresh longer.

Dry Quinoa:
It is important to store dry quinoa in a tightly sealed container and place it in a cool, dry place.

Cooked and Uneaten Quinoa:
Uneaten cooked quinoa should be stored in an airtight container and placed in the refrigerator.

Quinoa Flour:
Store the flour by putting it in an airtight container and keep in a refrigerator until you are ready to use it. I freeze quinoa flour for two to three months. (I have read that you can freeze quinoa flour for up to six months, but I always try to use mine within three months).

Quinoa Recipes

Quinoa Breads and Muffins

Delicious Quinoa Muffins

This muffin recipe is a staple in our home. We make them every week so that we have them for breakfast or snack.

Ingredients
1/2 cup uncooked quinoa
2 cups water
1/4 cup vegetable oil
2 cups all-purpose flour
3/4 cup dark brown sugar
1 1/2 teaspoon baking powder
1 teaspoon salt
1/2 cup raisins
3/4 cup milk
1 egg
1 teaspoon pure vanilla extract

Directions
Preheat oven to 350 degrees (F.)

Grease the bottom of a 12 muffin, muffin pan or use paper muffin cups.

Note: Rinse the quinoa seeds with water until water runs clear, prior to cooking.

In a medium pan, bring the water to a boil and add quinoa. Allow it to boil again and then cover. Continue to cook over medium heat for about 15 minutes or until the water was absorbed. Remove from heat and set aside to let cool.

In a medium bowl, stir together flour, sugar, baking powder, salt, raisins, and quinoa.

In a small bowl, whisk together oil, milk, egg, and vanilla.

Add milk mixture to flour mixture, and stir until combined. Fill muffin cups with batter, about 2/3 full.

Bake at 350 degrees (F.) for about 25-28 minutes or until toothpick inserted into the center of a muffin comes out clean.

Cool muffins in pan for about 5 minutes and then transfer to a wire rack to cool completely.

Makes 12 muffins.

Very Berry Quinoa Muffins

These muffins are delicious and have the added health benefits of blueberries.

Ingredients
2 eggs
1/2 cup quinoa flour
1/2 cup wheat flour
1/3 cup brown sugar
2 tablespoons honey
2 teaspoons baking powder
1 teaspoons baking soda
1/2 teaspoons salt
1/4 cup fresh blueberries

Directions
Preheat oven to 400 degrees (F).

In a large bowl, mix the flours and all dry ingredients.

Fold in the blueberries honey and eggs.

Pour into greased muffin tins, filling tins a little more than 1/2 full.

Bake 20 minutes or until lightly brown and toothpick stuck in center comes out clean.

Makes 12 muffins.

Bananaberry Quinoa Muffins

Most people prefer blueberry muffins, but these strawberry muffins are delicious as well. My family makes these often in June, right after spending the weekend strawberry picking at a local farm. Fresh strawberries really make these muffins fabulous!

Ingredients
1/3 cups quinoa flour
1 cup all-purpose flour
1 teaspoon baking powder
1/2 teaspoon salt
1/2 cup firmly packed brown sugar
2 eggs, lightly beaten
2 tablespoon melted butter
1 teaspoon vanilla extract
2 medium ripe bananas, mashed
1 cup cooked quinoa
1 1/2 cups chopped fresh strawberries

Directions
Preheat the oven to 375 degrees (F.)

Grease a muffin tin with cooking spray or use paper muffin liners.

In a medium bowl, mix together the flours, baking powder and salt.

In a large bowl, combine the brown sugar, butter, eggs & vanilla and whisk until smooth.

Take the flour mixture and a little at a time, add it to the sugar mixture and stir together until well mixed.

When all the flour has been mixed in, add the mashed bananas and the quinoa, and mix well.

Fold in the chopped strawberries into the muffin batter.

Divide the batter among the prepared muffin cups.

Bake for about 20-25 minutes or until a toothpick inserted into the center of one of the muffins comes out clean.

Remove from oven and cool for about 5 minutes before removing muffins from pan.

Cool on a rack for about 10 minutes, or until ready to serve. Makes 12 muffins.

Easy and Delicious Quinoa Bread

This is a delicious bread recipe for every day use. It is easy to make with just a few ingredients and is more satisfying than store bought bread. In this recipe you do not need to cook the quinoa first.

Ingredients
1 cup uncooked quinoa
2 cups warm water
1 tablespoon sugar
1 packet active dry yeast
1 teaspoon salt
2 cups whole wheat flour
1 1/2 cups all-purpose bread flour
2 tablespoons vegetable oil

Directions
Preheat oven to 400 degrees (F.)

Note: Rinse the quinoa seeds with water until water runs clear, prior to cooking.

Dissolve the packet of yeast in one cup of warm water. Add the sugar, stir and set aside. If mixture does not foam, start over with a new packet of yeast.

In a large bowl, mix wheat and all-purpose flour and salt. Mix in the quinoa.

To the flour mixture, add the yeast mixture. By hand mix and knead.

A little at a time, add the remaining warm water as you knead the dough. Use only enough to form the dough without it becoming runny.

Continue to knead the bread for 5 minutes.

Form the dough into round ball and place it in a large bowl.

Cover the dough ball in oil with your hands. Make sure that the entire outside of the dough is covered.

Cover the bowl with a towel and let it rise for 2 hours. The dough should double in size.

Punch the dough down, and knead it for two minutes.

Split the dough into two pieces. Form each piece into a loaf and place on a baking sheet that is lightly sprinkled with flour.

Allow them to sit for about 20 minutes. Bake the bread for 20 to 25 minutes. Allow it to cool completely before you start to cut it.

Yields two loaves of bread.

Tasty Cornbread With Quinoa

This recipe I have also included in my book, ***Quinoa Recipes for Weight Loss***. It is a family favorite and is a great snack or dinner side.

Ingredients
1 tablespoon butter, to grease pan
1 cup whole wheat flour
3/4 cup yellow cornmeal
1 teaspoon baking powder
1/2 teaspoon baking soda
2 eggs
1 1/2 cups cooked quinoa, cooled
3 tablespoon unsalted butter, melted and cooled
3 tablespoon brown sugar
3/4 teaspoon salt
2 cups milk
1 1/2 tablespoon white wine vinegar
1 cup heavy cream

Directions
Note: Rinse the quinoa seeds with water until water runs clear, prior to cooking.

Preheat an oven to 350 degrees (F).

Butter a 10-inch baking dish.

In a large bowl, mix together cornmeal, flour, baking soda, and baking powder.

In a medium-sized bowl, beat eggs and add melted butter, and quinoa. Mix well. Then stir in salt, vinegar, sugar, and milk.

Slowly add the wet ingredients to the dry ingredients and mix. Batter will be thin.

Pour batter into baking dish.

Pour cream into the middle of the batter. Do not stir mixture.

Place in the oven and bake 45 minutes.

Cornbread is done when the top is light brown.

Moist Nutty Zucchini Quinoa Bread

This is a moister version of the zucchini bread recipe that is in my ***Quinoa Recipes for Weight Loss*** book. After publishing that book, I tried different variations and this one is really tasty.

Ingredients
2 bananas, mashed
2 eggs
1/4 cups coconut milk
2 teaspoons vanilla extract
1 cup grated zucchini squash
1 1/2 cups quinoa flour
1 1/2 teaspoon baking powder
1/4 teaspoon salt
1 tablespoon cinnamon
1/2 cup chopped walnuts
1/2 cup honey

Directions
Preheat oven to 350 degrees (F).

Grease and flour one bread loaf pan. Set aside.

In a large bowl mix bananas, eggs, coconut milk and vanilla.

Add in the grated zucchini and mix well.

Add the quinoa flour, baking powder, salt and cinnamon. Mix well. Mix in the walnuts and honey. Mix batter thoroughly.

Pour the batter into loaf pan.

Bake for 45 minutes, or until a knife inserted into the center comes out clean.

Quinoa Bars

Extra Delicious Mocha Fudge Brownies

These delicious brownies are quick and easy to make! They are a favorite of my daughter's who loves the taste of coffee. To save time making this dish, I often cook the quinoa the day before and refrigerate until I'm ready to bake the brownies.

Ingredients
1/4 cup uncooked cooked quinoa
1 1/3 cup water
1/2 cup butter
8 ounces bittersweet or semisweet chocolate, coarsely chopped
1 teaspoon instant coffee
1/2 cup brown sugar
1/2 cup raw sugar
3 large eggs
1 teaspoon vanilla extract
3/4 cup all-purpose flour
1/2 teaspoon salt
6-8 ounces chocolate chips

Directions
Preheat the oven to 350 degrees (F.)

Lightly grease an 8-inch square baking pan.

Note: Rinse the quinoa seeds with water until water runs clear, prior to cooking.

In a medium pan, bring the water to a boil and add quinoa. Allow it to boil again and then cover. Continue to cook over medium heat for about 15 minutes or until the water was absorbed. Remove from heat and set aside to let cool.

In a medium bowl, mix the flour and salt together.

In a medium saucepan over medium heat, melt the butter and chocolate stirring until both are melted. When melted, add the coffee and mix well. Remove from heat and allow to cool.

In a large bowl, whisk together the eggs, sugars and vanilla until smooth. Mix in the melted chocolate. Taking a little flour at a time, fold in the flour until completely mixed. Once the flour has been mixed, carefully add the cooled cooked quinoa and chocolate chips. Mix well.

Pour the brownie batter into the greased baking pan and bake for 35-40 minutes or until a knife inserted into the middle comes out clean.

Allow to cool for 10-15 minutes before cutting.

ChocoCoconut Quinoa Brownies

The combination of dark chocolate and coconut make the taste of these brownies hard to beat!

Ingredients
1 cup all-purpose flour
1/2 cup quinoa flour
2 teaspoons baking powder
1 teaspoon salt
1 cup butter
8 ounces chopped dark chocolate
2 1/4 cup sugar
1 teaspoon vanilla extract
5 eggs
2/3 cup sweetened coconut flakes

Directions
Preheat oven to 350 degrees (F.)

Grease the bottom and sides of 13 x 9 inch pan.

In a large bowl combine the flours, baking powder and salt. Set aside.

In a saucepan, over low heat, melt the butter and chocolate together, stirring until chocolate is melted. Remove from heat. Stir in the vanilla and sugar.

In a large bowl, mix the chocolate mixture into the flour mixture. Add the eggs one at a time. Mix well.

Pour batter into the greased baking pan. Sprinkle the coconut on top.

Bake at 350 (F.) for 25-28 minutes. These bars will be slightly undone in the center, but will firm up after refrigeration.

It is best if you are able to refrigerate overnight before cutting, but usually 2 hours is enough, if you just can't wait overnight!

Nutty Dark Chocolate Bars

The combination of almond butter and honey really bring out the flavors in this chocolate bar snack.

Ingredients
1 cup almond butter
1/2 cup honey
2 eggs
1 teaspoon vanilla
1/2 cup quinoa flour
1 cup wheat flour
1/2 cup dark chocolate chips
1 teaspoon baking powder

Directions
Preheat oven to 350 degrees (F.)

Grease an 8" square baking pan.

In a large mixing bowl, combine all the wet ingredients together in a mixing bowl.

Stir in all of the dry ingredients.

Pour mixture the greased baking pan.

Bake 20 minutes or until knife inserted into the center comes out clean. Allow to cool completely before cutting. Makes 9-12 bars.

Flavor-Full Quinoa Bars

This quinoa bar is full of nutrition, flavor and texture.

Ingredients
1/2 cup raisins (and 1 cup warm water)
1/2 chopped walnuts
1/4 cup uncooked quinoa
1 1/3 cups water (to cook the quinoa)
1 cup packed brown sugar
1 cup rice flour
1 teaspoon baking powder
1/2 teaspoon baking soda
1 1/2 teaspoons ground cinnamon
1/2 teaspoon ground cloves
1/2 teaspoon ground nutmeg
1/2 cup chopped dates
1/2 cup butter, melted
3 large eggs
1/2 cup orange juice
2 teaspoons pure vanilla extract

Directions
Preheat the oven to 350 degrees (F.) Lightly grease a 9 x 9 inch pan. (For a thinner, crispier bar you can use a 13 x 9 inch pan and bake for 30 minutes).

Note: Rinse the quinoa seeds with water until water runs clear, prior to cooking.

In a medium pan, bring the water to a boil and add quinoa. Allow it to boil again and then cover. Continue to cook over medium heat for about 15 minutes or until the water was absorbed. Remove from heat and set aside to let cool.

In a cup of warm water, place the raisins for 10 minutes.

In a small pan over medium heat, toast the chopped walnuts for about 2 minutes.

In a large mixing bowl, combine the brown sugar, rice flour, baking powder, baking soda, cinnamon, cloves, nutmeg, dates, nuts and raisins. Mix well.

Mix the cooled cooked quinoa into the dry ingredient mixture.

To the quinoa mixture add the melted butter, eggs, orange juice and vanilla extract.

Pour the batter into the 13 x 9 inch pan.

Bake at 350 degrees (F.) for 35 minutes or until a knife inserted into the center comes out clean.

Makes 16 bars.

Peanutty Chocolate Quinoa Bars

If you love the taste of chocolate and peanut butter, these quinoa bars can't be beat! I love the addition of pecans – it makes the bars crunchy and flavorful!

Ingredients
1/2 cups uncooked quinoa
2 cups water
1/3 cup pecans
1/3 cup chocolate chips
2 tablespoons brown sugar
1 tablespoon honey
1 tablespoon vanilla extract
1 egg
Pinch of cinnamon
1/3 cup peanut butter

Directions
Preheat oven to 375 degrees (F.)

Note: Rinse the quinoa seeds with water until water runs clear, prior to cooking.

In a medium pan, bring the water to a boil and add quinoa. Allow it to boil again and then cover. Continue to cook over medium heat for about 15 minutes or until the water was absorbed. Remove from heat and set aside to let cool.

In a large mixing bowl, place cooked quinoa, pecans and chocolate chips.

In a small mixing bowl, mix together brown sugar, honey, vanilla, and egg.

Pour the quinoa mixture to the brown sugar mixture and mix well.

Add the cinnamon and peanut butter and mix again.

Spread mixture into 13” x 9” baking pan.

Bake for 20 minutes.

Cool completely before cutting. If sticky or runny, refrigerate for an hour before cutting. Makes 10-12 bars.

Quick and Easy Chocolate Quinoa Bars

These bars are easy to make, very healthy and filling. They are a fabulous substitute for store-bought granola bars.

Ingredients
1/3 cups uncooked quinoa
1 1/2 cups water
4 dates (chopped up for ease in mixing)
2 tablespoon cocoa powder
1 1/2 teaspoon coconut oil
1/4 cup chocolate chips

Directions
Preheat oven to 375 degrees (F.)

Note: Rinse the quinoa seeds with water until water runs clear, prior to cooking.

In a medium pan, bring the water to a boil and add quinoa. Allow it to boil again and then cover. Continue to cook over medium heat for about 15 minutes or until the water was absorbed. Remove from heat and set aside to let cool.

In a large bowl, place all the ingredients and combine well.

Spread onto a cookie sheet about 1-inch thick.

Bake for 25 minutes. Cool completely before cutting into bars. Makes 8-10 bars.

Touch of Maple Quinoa Bars

I make these bars often, as the few ingredients are always readily available. I can whip up a batch on a moment's notice.

Ingredients
1/2 cups uncooked quinoa
2 cups water
4 eggs, beaten
1/3 cup vanilla soy milk
1/3 cup maple syrup
1 teaspoon vanilla extract
1 tablespoon cinnamon

Directions
Preheat oven to 375 degrees (F).

Note: Rinse the quinoa seeds with water until water runs clear, prior to cooking.

In a medium pan, bring the water to a boil and add quinoa. Allow it to boil again and then cover. Continue to cook over medium heat for about 15 minutes or until the water was absorbed. Remove from heat and set aside to let cool.

Lightly grease an 8-inch square baking pan and line with parchment paper.

In a small bowl, whisk together eggs, soy milk, vanilla extract, and cinnamon. Add the maple syrup and mix.

In a large bowl, combine the cooked quinoa and egg mixture. Stir until well mixed.

Pour the mixture into the baking dish.

Bake for 20 to 25 minutes until golden brown.

Carefully remove the bake from the pan, using the parchment paper.

Allow to cool completely before cutting it into bars.

Quinoa Cookies

Old Time Favorite Quinoa Cookies

These cookies, made with quinoa and flax seeds add lots of healthy nutrients to everyone's favorite cookie!

Ingredients
1/3 cup uncooked quinoa
2 cups water
1 cup muesli
1/2 cup quinoa flour
1 cup whole wheat flour
1 1/4 cup applesauce
1 1/4 cup brown sugar
8 ounces chocolate chips

1 teaspoon baking soda
1 teaspoon salt
1 1/2 tablespoons ground flax seeds
1/4 cup tablespoons water

Directions
Preheat oven to 375 degrees (F).

Note: Rinse the quinoa seeds with water until water runs clear, prior to cooking.

In a medium pan, bring the water (2 cups) to a boil and add quinoa. Allow it to boil again and then cover. Continue to cook over medium heat for about 15 minutes or until the water was absorbed. Remove from heat and set aside to let cool.

In a small bowl, combine ground flax seeds with water (1/4 cup) and set aside.

In a large bowl, sift together quinoa flour, wheat flour, baking soda, and salt.

In another large bowl combine applesauce and brown sugar. To this add the flax seed mixture and mix well. Add in the dry ingredient mixture and stir well.

Add the quinoa, muesli and chocolate chips.

Line two baking sheets with parchment paper. Drop cookies by the spoonful on the baking sheets. Bake for 10-12 minutes or until golden brown. Makes 24 cookies.

Gooey Peanut Butter and Quinoa Cookies

Ingredients
1/4 cup uncooked quinoa
2 cups water
1/3 cup brown sugar
1/2 cup butter
1/2 cup peanut butter
1/2 cup honey
1 cup rice flour
1/4 teaspoon salt
1 teaspoon baking soda

Directions
Preheat oven to 350 degrees (F).

Note: Rinse the quinoa seeds with water until water runs clear, prior to cooking.

In a medium pan, bring the water to a boil and add quinoa. Allow it to boil again and then cover. Continue to cook over medium heat for about 15 minutes or until the water was absorbed. Remove from heat and set aside to let cool.

In a large mixing bowl, combine the brown sugar, butter, peanut butter and honey and mix until creamy.

To this mixture add the remaining ingredients and mix well.

Place spoonfuls of batter onto cookie sheets. Bake for 10 – 12 minutes.

Makes 2 dozen cookies.

Quinoa Oatmeal Chewies

These cookies are my favorites! I love oatmeal cookies, and because of the nutty flavor of quinoa, it makes this classic cookie even more delicious! I make at least one batch of these cookies every week!

Ingredients
1/4 cup uncooked quinoa
1 1/3 cup water
1/2 cup oatmeal
1 cup all-purpose flour
1/3 cup sugar
4 tablespoons canola oil
1/4 cup vanilla soymilk

Directions
Preheat oven to 350 degrees (F.)

Note: Rinse the quinoa seeds with water until water runs clear, prior to cooking.

In a medium pan, bring the water to a boil and add quinoa. Allow it to boil again and then cover. Continue to cook over medium heat for about 15 minutes or until the water was absorbed. Remove from heat and set aside to let cool.

In a large bowl, mix oatmeal, flour and sugar. Add the oil and soymilk. Mix well. Fold in the quinoa and then mix until all ingredients are combined.

Line two baking sheets with parchment paper. Place spoonfuls of batter onto cookie sheets.

For chewy cookies, bake for 10 minutes. For crispier cookies, bake 12 minutes.

Makes 24 cookies.

Quinoa Cakes

Melt-In-Your-Mouth Chocolate Cupcakes

These cupcakes are rich, moist and delicious! It is impossible to stop with just one! You can also use this recipe to make a cake, just use two 8" round pans, grease and flour the pans, divide the batter and bake for about 40 minutes or until a knife inserted in the center comes out clean.

Ingredients for Cake
2/3 cup uncooked quinoa
2 cups water
1/3 cup milk
4 large eggs
1 teaspoon pure vanilla extract
3/4 cup butter melted
1 1/2 cups sugar
1 cup cocoa powder
1 1/2 teaspoon baking powder
1/2 teaspoon baking soda
1/2 teaspoon salt

Ingredients for Frosting
1/2 cup whipping cream
4 ounces bittersweet chocolate

Directions
Preheat over to 350 degrees (F.)

Grease the bottom of a cupcake/muffin pan or use paper muffin liners.

Note: Rinse the quinoa seeds with water until water runs clear, prior to cooking.

In a medium pan, bring the water to a boil and add quinoa. Allow it to boil again and then cover. Continue to cook over medium heat for about 15 minutes or until the water was absorbed. Remove from heat and set aside to let cool.

In a blender, blend the milk, eggs and vanilla. Add the quinoa and butter. Blend again until smooth.

In a medium bowl, mix the sugar, cocoa, baking powder, baking soda and salt. Add the blender mixture and mix well.

Fill cupcake tins a little more than half full. Place tin on the center over rack and bake for 18-20 minutes or until a knife inserted in the center comes out clean or they spring back when lightly touched.

Remove the cake from the oven and cool completely before topping with your favorite frosting.

Directions for Frosting
In a medium saucepan pour the cream and heat until hot.

In a glass bowl (or a bowl that can withstand heat) place the chocolate. Pour the hot cream over the chocolate and whisk until smooth and creamy. Drizzle over cupcakes.

Makes 12 cupcakes.

Cinnamon Apple Quinoa Cake

This is a fabulous breakfast or midafternoon snack cake! It is very filling and nutrient rich!

Ingredients for Cake
1/3 cup uncooked quinoa
1 cup of water
3/4 cup whole wheat flour
1/2 teaspoon baking powder
1/4 teaspoon baking soda
1/2 teaspoon ground ginger
1/2 teaspoon ground cinnamon
1/4 teaspoon salt
1 large apple, cored and coarsely grated
1/4 cup sugar
1/4 cup olive oil
1 teaspoon vanilla extract
3 tablespoons sunflower seeds
1/4 cup raisins

Ingredients for Cinnamon Topping
1/4 cup rolled oats
1 teaspoon ground cinnamon
1 tablespoon sugar
1 tablespoon olive oil

Directions
Preheat oven to 350 degrees (F.)

Grease a loaf pan.

Note: Rinse the quinoa seeds with water until water runs clear, prior to cooking.

In a medium pan, bring the water to a boil and add quinoa. Allow it to boil again and then cover. Continue to cook over medium heat for about 15 minutes or until the water was absorbed. Remove from heat and set aside to let cool.

In a large bowl, sift together flour, sugar, baking powder, soda, ginger, cinnamon and salt. Set aside.

In a medium bowl, mix the grated apple, oil, quinoa, vanilla, sunflower seeds and raisins. Add the wet ingredients to dry ingredients and stir until combined.

Pour the mixture into the loaf pan and level the top.

Directions for Topping
In a small bowl combine the topping ingredients: the rolled oats, cinnamon, sugar and olive oil. Mix them well and then sprinkle them on top of the cake batter.

Place cake on the center rack of the oven at 350 degrees (F.) and bake for 30-40 minutes, until cake comes out clean with the clean knife test. Let cool before cutting into slices.

Spicy Quinoa Cake

This is a healthier version of the classic spice cake. It is also very moist and flavorful!

Ingredients for Cake
1/2 cup uncooked quinoa
1 1/3 cups water
1/2 cup vegetable oil
1 1/4 cups packed dark brown sugar
3 eggs
2 teaspoons grated orange rind
2 1/4 cups whole wheat flour, sifted
1 1/2 teaspoon baking powder
1/2 teaspoon ground cinnamon
1/4 teaspoon ground cloves
1/3 cup milk
dash of salt

Ingredients for Frosting
1 package of low-fat cream cheese (12 ounce size)
1/2 cup confectioners' sugar
1 1/2 teaspoon vanilla extract

Directions for Cake
Preheat oven to 350 degrees (F.)

Note: Rinse the quinoa seeds with water until water runs clear, prior to cooking.

In a medium pan, bring the cup of water to a boil and add quinoa. Allow it to boil again and then cover. Continue to cook over medium heat for about 15 minutes or until the water was absorbed. Remove from heat and set aside to let cool.

In a medium mixing bowl, mix oil, sugar and orange rind. Slowly add each egg, one at a time, beating each egg well into the mixture.

In another bowl, mix all of the remaining dry ingredients. Slowly add the sugar mixture and milk, alternating a little of each as you mix.

Stir in the cooked quinoa and mix well.

Pour the mixture into a greased and floured 9" x 13" pan at 350 degrees (F.) for 40 minutes.

Directions for Frosting
In a medium mixing bowl, combine cream cheese, sugar and vanilla. Using an electric mixer beat until smooth and creamy. When the cake has completely cooled, frost the cake. Refrigerate the cake after frosting and if there is any left over after serving. In our family, this is never the case!

Easy Maple Quinoa Hot Cakes

Ok, I have to come clean on this recipe. It is not a 'baked' recipe. This is my family's favorite pancake recipe. I added it here because they insisted. We make these hotcakes often, sometimes for breakfast, but just as often for a snack or dessert. So under pressure from them, I have included it here. I hope you enjoy them as much as we do!

Ingredients
1/3 uncooked quinoa
1 cup water
3/4 cup all-purpose flour
2 teaspoons baking powder
1/2 teaspoon coarse salt
1 large egg whites
1 tablespoon unsalted butter, melted
1/4 cup low-fat milk
2 tablespoons maple syrup
fresh fruit of your choice (I prefer blueberries).

Directions

Note: Rinse the quinoa seeds with water until water runs clear, prior to cooking.

In a medium pan, bring the water to a boil and add quinoa. Allow it to boil again and then cover. Continue to cook over medium heat for about 15 minutes or until the water was absorbed. Remove from heat and set aside to let cool.

In a medium bowl, whisk together quinoa, flour, baking powder, and salt.

In a second bowl, whisk together egg, egg white, butter, milk, and syrup until smooth.

Slowly add the egg mixture to the flour mixture and mix well.

Lightly coat a large nonstick skillet with non-stick spray or a pat of butter. Heat over medium-high. Drop batter with a tablespoon onto the hot skillet.

Cook until bubbles appear on top, about 2 minutes. Flip cakes and cook until golden brown on underside, another 2 minutes. Wipe skillet clean and repeat by adding more non-stick spray or melted butter. Continue with remaining batter. Serve with maple syrup and fresh fruit.

Conclusion

Quinoa has become my favorite ingredient for making breakfast, lunch and dinner dishes, and now for desserts too! Since quinoa packs so many nutrients, you can easily make every day desserts and snacks healthier in very delicious ways.

I often make the quinoa ahead of time so that I have it on hand when I am ready to bake. The more you use and become comfortable with baking with quinoa the more you will see how easy it is to incorporate it into your favorite dessert recipes!

Here's to healthier eating!

~Sarah

3790583R00031

Printed in Great Britain
by Amazon.co.uk, Ltd.,
Marston Gate.